States
ILLINOIS

by Angie Swanson

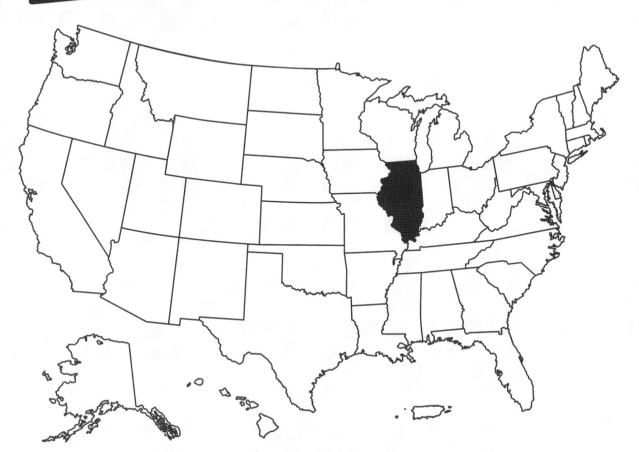

CAPSTONE PRESS
a capstone imprint

Next Page Books are published by Capstone Press,
1710 Roe Crest Drive, North Mankato, Minnesota 56003
www.mycapstone.com

Library of Congress Cataloging-in-Publication Data
Cataloging-in-publication information is on file with the Library of
Congress.
ISBN 978-1-5157-0399-0 (library binding)
ISBN 978-1-5157-0459-1 (paperback)
ISBN 978-1-5157-0511-6 (ebook PDF)

Editorial Credits
Jaclyn Jaycox, editor; Kazuko Collins and Katy LaVigne, designers;
Morgan Walters, media researcher; Laura Manthe, production specialist

Photo Credits
Capstone Press: Angi Gahler, map 4, 7; Corbis: GraphicaArtis,
12; Getty Images: Hulton Archive, top 19; Glow Images: Heritage
Images, 26; Library of Congress: Prints and Photographs Division
Washington, D.C., 27; National Geographic Creative: IRA BLOCK, 10;
Newscom: Everett Collection, middle 19, Ken Welsh, 25, Sportswire,
29; North Wind Picture Archives, top 18; One Mile Up, Inc., flag, seal
23; Shutterstock: Anthony Correia, bottom 24, anthony heflin, 7,
ArturNyk, top 24, BluIz60, top left 21, Connie Barr, bottom left 20,
f11photo, 17, gary718, 28, Helga Esteb, bottom 19, Henryk Sadura, 13,
isoga, middle right 21, Jason Patrick Ross, 11, middle left 21, bottom
right 21, Joseph Sohm, 5, 16, 18, Kelly Marken, 14, Mark Baldwin,
bottom right 8, Matt Jeppson, top right 21, Natalia Ganelin, top right
20, Neveshkin Nikolay, middle 18, Nicholas Courtney, bottom left 8,
nito, 15, Rudy Balasko, 9, SergiyN, cover, Tom Reichner, bottom right
20, Tupungato, 6, Weldon Schloneger, bottom left 21; Wikimedia:
Jyamuca, top left 20

All design elements by Shutterstock

Printed and bound in China.
0316/CA21600187
012016   009436F16

TABLE OF CONTENTS

Want to take your research further? Ask your librarian if your school subscribes to PebbleGo Next. If so, when you see this helpful symbol ⟳ throughout the book, log onto www.pebblegonext.com for bonus downloads and information.

LOCATION

Illinois is one of the nation's midwestern states. Wisconsin lies to the north. On the east are Lake Michigan and Indiana. Kentucky lies south of Illinois. To the west are Iowa and Missouri. The Mississippi River runs along the western edge of Illinois. The Wabash and Ohio rivers form part of the eastern border. Chicago, the largest city in Illinois, rises along the shore of Lake Michigan. After Chicago, the state's biggest cities are Aurora, Rockford, Joliet, and Naperville.

PebbleGo Next Bonus!
To print and label your own map, go to www.pebblegonext.com and search keywords:

Legend
⊗ Capital
• City
  Lake
  River

4

Chicago is the third-largest city in the United States, with a population of more than 2.7 million.

GEOGRAPHY

Three main land regions are found in Illinois. The Shawnee Hills is a narrow region in southern Illinois. Trees cover the hilly land. The Shawnee National Forest covers a large part of this area. The Gulf Coastal Plain region is at the state's southern edge. The Mississippi River forms the western border of this area. The Ohio River lies to the east. The broad, flat land of the Central Plains covers 90 percent of the state. Near this region's northwestern corner, the state's highest point, Charles Mound, rises 1,235 feet (376 meters).

PebbleGo Next Bonus! To watch a video about the Old State Capital, go to www.pebblegonext.com and search keywords:

IL VIDEO

The Chicago River is 156 miles (251 kilometers) long and runs through the city of Chicago.

Rock formations in the Garden of the Gods, Shawnee National Forest

Charles Mound

Lake Michigan

Des Plaines River

Chicago River

Mississippi River

Illinois River

CENTRAL PLAINS

Cahokia Mounds

Carlyle Lake

Mississippi River

SHAWNEE HILLS

GULF COASTAL PLAIN

Ohio River

Legend

▲ Highest Point

⬭ Lake

○ Point of Interest

〰 River

Scale

Miles

0 20   40   60   80

0 20 40 60 80 100

Kilometers

WEATHER

Illinois has cold winters and warm summers. The average winter temperature is 29 degrees Fahrenheit (minus 1.7 degrees Celsius). The average summer temperature is 74°F (23°C).

Average High and Low Temperatures (Chicago, IL)

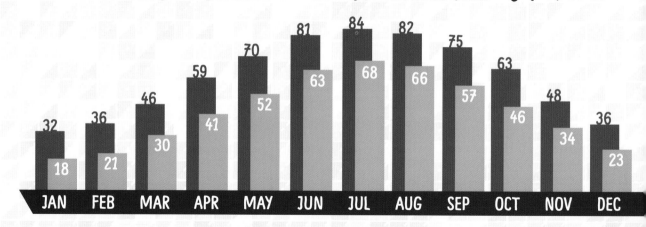

	JAN	FEB	MAR	APR	MAY	JUN	JUL	AUG	SEP	OCT	NOV	DEC
High	32	36	46	59	70	81	84	82	75	63	48	36
Low	18	21	30	41	52	63	68	66	57	46	34	23

LANDMARKS

Willis Tower

The Willis Tower in downtown Chicago is one of the world's tallest buildings. It has 110 stories and is 1,450 feet (442 m) high. The building was formerly named the Sears Tower. Visitors ride an elevator to the observatory on the 103rd floor. On a clear day, they can see four states — Illinois, Indiana, Michigan, and Wisconsin.

Cahokia Mounds

At the Cahokia Mounds in southern Illinois, visitors climb to the top of Monks Mound to imagine how the ancient city looked. Monks Mound is the largest American Indian mound in the country. Many mounds likely served as bases for temples and as leaders' homes.

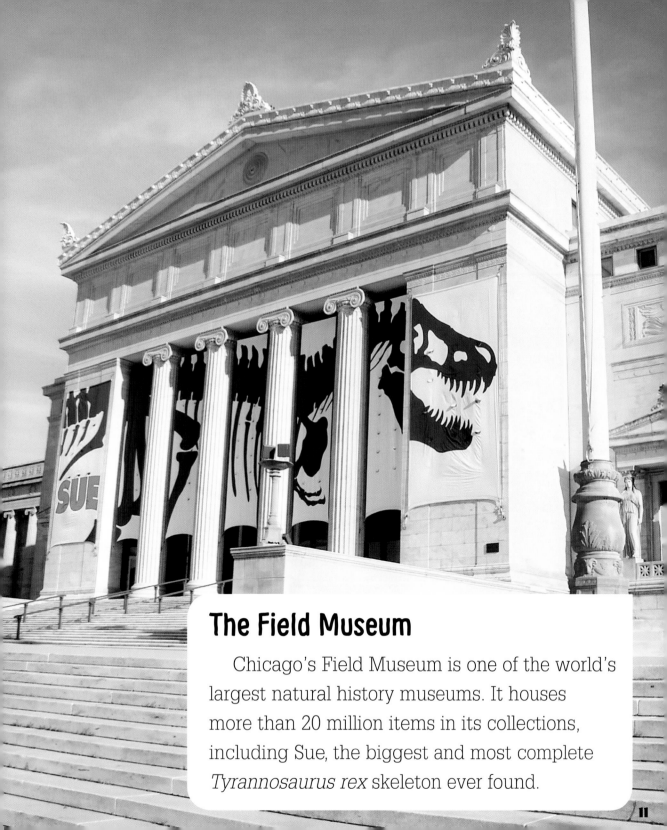

The Field Museum

Chicago's Field Museum is one of the world's largest natural history museums. It houses more than 20 million items in its collections, including Sue, the biggest and most complete *Tyrannosaurus rex* skeleton ever found.

Explorers Jacques Marquette and Louis Jolliet travel down the Mississippi River in 1673.

Before French settlers arrived, American Indians lived on the Illinois prairie. In 1673 French explorers Louis Jolliet and Father Jacques Marquette traveled south along the present-day border of Illinois. Then in 1717 Illinois became part of the French colony of Louisiana. After the British won the French and Indian wars in 1763, the Illinois region came under British control. In 1783 American colonists won the Revolutionary War against Great Britain. The Illinois region then became part of the United States. In 1818 Illinois became the 21st state.

Illinois' state government is made up of three branches. The governor leads the executive branch, which carries out laws. The legislature is made up of the 59-member Senate and the 118-member House of Representatives. They make the laws for Illinois. Judges and their courts make up the judicial branch.

Illinois' state capitol building is located in Springfield.

INDUSTRY

Like most states, Illinois has a mixed economy. It is a top agricultural state, but manufacturing, mining, and service industries also add to the state's wealth. Farms cover most of Illinois' land. Crops account for about 85 percent of the state's total agricultural income. Corn and soybeans are Illinois' top crops. Illinois grows more soybeans than any other state. It is also a leading producer of hogs. Illinois' coal beds are the richest in the country.

More than 9 million acres (3.6 million hectares) of soybeans are planted each year in Illinois.

The state also mines limestone, clay, and gravel. Farm equipment is an important Illinois product. Processed foods and many kinds of chemicals are made in Illinois too.

Today most Illinois workers have service jobs. Some work in hospitals, hotels, and restaurants. Others are teachers, lawyers, store clerks, or bankers.

The Illinois Coal Basin covers 65 percent of Illinois.

POPULATION

Most of the people in Illinois are white. More than 8 million white people live in the state. Nearly 2 million of Illinois' residents are African-American. Few African-Americans lived in Illinois before the Civil War. Many African-Americans arrived between World War I and World War II to work in Illinois factories.

Today Illinois is attracting people from Spanish-speaking areas and Asia. Many are moving to suburbs near Chicago and other cities. About 2 million Hispanics live in Illinois. Fairmont City has a growing number of Hispanic people.

Population by Ethnicity

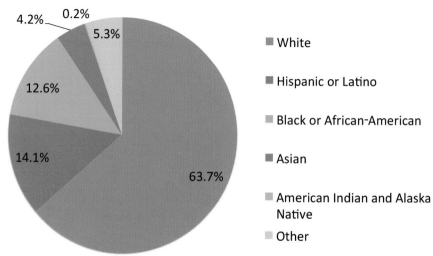

- White — 63.7%
- Hispanic or Latino — 14.1%
- Black or African-American — 12.6%
- Asian — 4.2%
- American Indian and Alaska Native — 0.2%
- Other — 5.3%

Source: U.S. Census Bureau.

About a half million people in Illinois are Asian. Naperville, near Chicago, has a large Asian population. Across Illinois, people continue to arrive from India, Korea, China, Pakistan, and other Asian countries.

FAMOUS PEOPLE

Black Hawk (1767–1838) was a Sauk Indian leader. He led the Sauk and Fox Indian tribes in a fight to keep their land in Illinois, which was later called the Black Hawk War (1832). He and his followers were defeated. He was born near the mouth of the Rock River in northwestern Illinois.

Abraham Lincoln (1809–1865) was the 16th president of the United States (1861–1865). He issued the Emancipation Proclamation, granting freedom to slaves. He was born in Kentucky and began his career in Springfield.

Ronald Reagan (1911–2004) was the 40th president of the United States (1981–1989). Before becoming president, he was a Hollywood actor who appeared in more than 50 films. He was born in Tampico.

Walt Disney (1901–1966) made animated cartoons and movies. He opened the Disneyland and Disney World amusement parks. He was born in Chicago.

Gwendolyn Brooks (1917–2000) was an American poet. In 1950 she became the first African-American to receive a Pulitzer Prize. She wrote more than 20 books of poetry throughout her career. She was born in Kansas and grew up in Chicago.

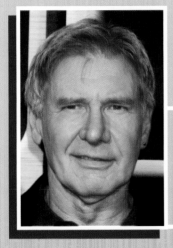

Harrison Ford (1942–) is a popular actor. His movies include the *Star Wars* and the *Indiana Jones* series. He was born in Chicago.

STATE SYMBOLS

Tree

white oak

Flower

violet

Bird

cardinal

Animal

white-tailed deer

PebbleGo Next Bonus! To make a dessert using cider from an important fruit crop in Illinois, go to www.pebblegonext.com and search keywords:

IL RECIPE

Folk Dance

square dance

Amphibian

eastern tiger salamander

Reptile

painted turtle

Fish

bluegill

Prairie Grass

big bluestem

Insect

monarch butterfly

FAST FACTS

STATEHOOD
1818

CAPITAL ☆
Springfield

LARGEST CITY •
Chicago

SIZE
55,519 square miles (143,794 square kilometers) land area (2010 U.S. Census Bureau)

POPULATION
12,882,135 (2013 U.S. Census estimate)

STATE NICKNAME
Prairie State

STATE MOTTO
"State Sovereignty, National Union"

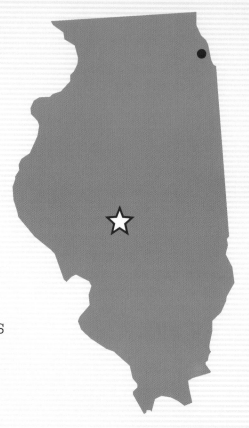

STATE SEAL

On the seal, an eagle sits on a boulder. The state motto, "State Sovereignty, National Union," is on the banner in the eagle's beak. A shield with 13 stars and stripes leans against the boulder. The stars and stripes stand for the 13 original states. A rising sun and a lake stand for progress. The date, Aug. 26th 1818, appears at the bottom of the seal. It is the day the first Illinois constitution was signed.

PebbleGo Next Bonus!
To print and color your own flag, go to www.pebblegonext.com and search keywords:

 IL FLAG

STATE FLAG

The Illinois state flag shows the Great Seal of Illinois on a white background. The seal shows a bald eagle with a banner in its mouth. On the banner is the state motto, "State Sovereignty, National Union." In the eagle's claws is a shield with 13 stars and stripes. They stand for the first 13 U.S. states. The eagle stands on a stone that shows two dates. One is 1818, which is the year Illinois became a state. The other is 1868, when the state seal was adopted. The ground beneath the eagle represents Illinois' rich prairie soil. The word "Illinois" appears below the seal.

MINING PRODUCTS

coal, petroleum, limestone, sand and gravel

MANUFACTURED GOODS

machinery, food products, chemicals, petroleum and coal products, computer and electronic equipment, plastics and rubber products

FARM PRODUCTS

corn, soybeans, wheat, sorghum, hay, hogs, beef cattle

PROFESSIONAL SPORTS TEAMS

Chicago Cubs (MLB)
Chicago White Sox (MLB)
Chicago Fire (MLS)
Chicago Bulls (NBA)
Chicago Sky (WNBA)
Chicago Bears (NFL)
Chicago Blackhawks (NHL)

PebbleGo Next Bonus! To learn the lyrics to the state song, go to www.pebblegonext.com and search keywords:

IL SONG

ILLINOIS TIMELINE

1620 — The Pilgrims establish a colony in the New World in present-day Massachusetts.

1673 — The Illinois Confederacy of American Indians lives in Illinois; French explorers Louis Jolliet and Father Jacques Marquette reach Illinois along the Mississippi River.

1699 — French priests set up Cahokia, the first town in Illinois.

1717 — Illinois becomes part of Louisiana, a French colony.

1763 France loses Illinois to Great Britain after Great Britain wins the French and Indian wars.

1775–1783 American colonists fight for their independence from Great Britain in the Revolutionary War.

1778 American Lieutenant Colonel George Rogers Clark's forces capture the Illinois towns of Cahokia and Kaskaskia from the British during the Revolutionary War.

1783 The Illinois region becomes part of the United States under the treaty ending the Revolutionary War.

1818 Illinois becomes the 21st state on December 3.

1858 — Illinois politicians Abraham Lincoln and Stephen Douglas hold famous debates on slavery as they campaign for a U.S. Senate seat.

1861–1865 — The Union and the Confederacy fight the Civil War. Illinois fights for the Union. About 250,000 Union soldiers from Illinois fight during the Civil War.

1871 — Fire destroys much of Chicago, killing at least 300 people and causing millions of dollars of damage. The fire leaves almost one-third of Chicago's residents homeless.

1893 — Chicago holds the World's Columbian Exposition, also known as the Chicago World's Fair. The fair celebrates the 400th anniversary of Christopher Columbus' landing in America.

1955 Ray Kroc opens his first McDonald's restaurant in Des Plaines, Illinois.

1968 The Democratic National Convention is held in Chicago. More than 500 people are arrested during the convention for protesting the Vietnam War (1954–1975).

1973 The Sears Tower in downtown Chicago is completed, becoming the world's tallest building at the time.

1983 Chicago native Harold Washington becomes Chicago's first African-American mayor.

1997 Chicago's Field Museum acquires Sue, the largest *Tyrannosaurus rex* skeleton ever found.

2009 Barack Obama of Illinois takes office as the first African-American president of the United States.

2011 Oprah Winfrey records her final show in Chicago, ending her daily talk shows after 25 years.

2015 The Chicago Blackhawks win their third Stanley Cup in six years.

Glossary

ethnicity *(ETH-niss-ih-tee)*—a group of people who share the same physical features, beliefs, and backgrounds

executive *(ig-ZE-kyuh-tiv)*—the branch of government that makes sure laws are followed

industry *(IN-duh-stree)*—a business which produces a product or provides a service

legislature *(LEJ-iss-lay-chur)*—a group of elected officials who have the power to make or change laws for a country or state

limestone *(LIME-stohn)*—hard rock used in building; made from the remains of ancient sea creatures

observatory *(uhb-ZUR-vuh-tor-ee)*—a building containing telescopes and other scientific instruments for studying the sky and the stars

petroleum *(puh-TROH-lee-uhm)*—an oily liquid found below the earth's surface used to make gasoline, heating oil, and many other products

prairie *(PRAIR-ee)*—a large area of flat or rolling grassland with few or no trees

region *(REE-juhn)*—a large area

Read More

Ganeri, Anita. *United States of America: A Benjamin Blog and His Inquisitive Dog Guide.* Country Guides. Chicago: Heinemann Raintree, 2015.

Marciniak, Kristin. *What's Great About Illinois?* Our Great States. Minneapolis: Lerner Publications, 2015.

Price-Groff, Claire. *Illinois.* It's My State! New York: Cavendish Square Publishing, 2015.

Internet Sites

FactHound offers a safe, fun way to find Internet sites related to this book. All of the sites on FactHound have been researched by our staff.

Here's all you do:

Visit *www.facthound.com*

Type in this code: 9781515703990

Super-cool stuff! Check out projects, games and lots more at **www.capstonekids.com**

Critical Thinking Using the Common Core

1. Who was Gwendolyn Brooks? List three things about her using the text. (Key Ideas and Details)

2. Chicago is one of the biggest cities in the United States. Describe ways a large population can affect tourism, jobs, crime, and pollution. (Integration of Knowledge and Ideas)

3. Petroleum is manufactured in Illinois. What is petroleum? Hint: Use the glossary to help with your answer. (Craft and Structure)

Index